Cryptocurrency Trading

Effective Strategies Bible for
Beginners and Advances that Are
Eager to Mastering this Lucrative
World and Earning Their First Million
Bucks

Table of Contents

Book description:

Today is the perfect time to do the Cryptocurrency trading or trading with the digital currency. It is awesome, it is something more than the money and is filled with the opportunities. The technology of Cryptocurrency carries a lot of benefits itself. Once they came in our economic environment, they were misunderstood and many buyers did a lot of mistakes due to many misconceptions and lack of knowledge.

The more information you have, more will be success. More you work hard, more you will enjoy. So, get this book and gather all the information you need to do Cryptocurrency trading and find the best opportunities hidden in this Cryptocurrency. Before starting the process, you need to know where to start with, how to start it, what mistakes you should avoid, and how to progress further.

This book will help you in understanding the concept in an easier way. Starting with the basics, here is the complete information about the pump and dumps of the Cryptocurrencies along with the future of this technology.

Copyrights:

The information in this document is indicated to be consistent and truthful, any liability for inattention or abusive use of this data will completely belong to the reader. Under no conditions will any blame or legal responsibility be believed against the editor or publisher for any monetary loss, damages or reparation due to the text and information, either direction and indirectly.

Respective authors have all copyrights not apprehended by the editor or publishers.

The details herein are for information purpose only and the presentation of this information is without any guarantee assurance or contract.

All brands and trademarks in this book are for clarification purposes and owned by the owners only. They are not affiliated with the document.

Introduction:

Cryptocurrencies are no more a part of the world of fantasy. It revolves around technology of using money in its digital form, rediscovering the conventional methods of finance and social business, while gathering millions of individuals from all over the world to a unique global economic center. Cryptocurrency assure the promising future of the financial status of a middle man.

Bitcoin, being a famous of all the Cryptocurrencies, brings the stability and flexibility of the process of the Cryptocurrency trading. Few people think that this system is going to eliminate the whole scenario of jobs and leaving them with the great deal of unemployment. Though the rumors are still to be answered.

To have a complete and sound knowledge of the fundamentals of Cryptocurrency and Cryptocurrency trading, this book includes complete package of a profound research on this field. Regardless of your own knowledge about the Cryptocurrency, there is much more to be dug in the market. Without knowing the trends of market, you can't take a single step. For learning each of the detail, you need to understand the basics and most importantly the future trends of this technology.

Other than this you will find following things in this book:

- An easy guide to know the block chain technology and the fundamentals of the Cryptocurrency trading.
- The details of the ways to get the Cryptocurrencies and the safe methods of saving them.
- A detailed information about the types of the Cryptocurrencies.

- The ways of starting the Cryptocurrency trading and how to perform the effective steps.
- When to trade and when to stop.
- Tools and platforms to trade Cryptocurrency
- Mistakes to be avoided
- And much more...

Chapter 01: What is cryptocurrency and how that works?

Basically a crypto currency which is commonly known as crypto currency usually used for electronic means of transactions.it ensures the transfer of assets and regulate the additional units. They are categorized under the division of digital currencies. Usually they are termed as virtual or alternative currencies.

In 2009, the very first cryptocurrency was introduced, named as bit coin. After this various other crypto currency were introduced which were called as bit coin alternative or altcoins. Bit coins and its related electronic money work opposite to the centralized electronic monetary systems. As a distributed ledger, bit coin work as bit coins block chain database transaction.

A well-known, decentralized cryptocurrency is created by the collaboration of whole cryptocurrency systems. On the other hand, the centralized banking and other economic systems like governments, Federal Reserve System or corporate bodies regulate the exchange of currency via printing fiat units of money or by other way, they enhance the electronic banking ledgers.

Contrary to centralized cryptocurrency, governments or companies are not allowed to create new units. Moreover, they are forbidden to support banks, firms or corporate bodies which contain some asset tenets in them. Decentralized crypto currencies basically based upon fundamental technical systems which can be in form of individual or group, called as Satoshi Nakamoto.

Until now 2017, thousands of cryptocurrency were hosted but more or less they appear similar to very first decentralized cryptocurrency, that is, bit coin. In cryptocurrency systems, miners; participants of general public who use electronic means to authorize the transactions and then sum up them in ledger as per time stamping scheme, tend to control the balance, security and integrity of ledgers. Monetary incentives are provided to miners for sustaining cryptocurrency ledger.

The major purpose of creating crypto currencies is to keep an eye on circulating currency and imitating expensive metals and lowering production of currency. As per law enforcements, crypto currencies are valuable then cash in hand or other financial institutions because it is hard to capture it. It is driven by cryptographic expertise. Silk Road case is one of the most prominent example.

Grafting of Cryptocurrency:

Cryptocurrency is encoded type of decentralize electronic currency which is confirmed in public ledger by a process known as mining. We will also discuss the functioning of crypto currencies such as bit coin. For this purpose, we have to take a look on fundamentals of crypto currency, later we will discuss some other properties of crypto currency.

Fundamentals of cryptocurrency:

Here are given some elementary terms and concepts about the working of crypto currency.

Public Ledgers:

It contains records of all transactions from the very beginning of creation of crypto currency. The system checks the legitimacy of record keeping by encrypting the identities of coin owners through cryptographic techniques. The digital wallets can measure accurate balance expenditures which are further assured by ledger. In addition, the transactions are reviewed to check whether the coin is owned by the spender. Cyptocurrency named a public ledger as "transaction block chain".

Transactions:

The trading of capitals among two digital wallets is known as transaction. After trading, the transactions are submerged into public ledger to wait for confirmation. The transitions are made, the trend of cryptographic signature begins with the passage of time and got a marked name because in this way people are made ensure about the transaction and money is directly coming from investor's pocket. Although it takes some time around 10 to 12 minutes particularly for bit coin, in this duration the miners confirm their transaction and sum up them in public ledger.

Mining:

It is simply defining as the confirmation of transactions and summing them in public ledger. For this purpose, first of all miner system will have to sort out complex electronic problems just like solving a mathematical puzzle. It is always kept open to all people so any one can easily check their transaction. Basic step of solving a puzzle is to create block of transaction in a ledger. It makes a perfect collaboration of blocks, transaction and block chain ledger in such a way that no one can edit them as per their own will.

When it creates a block in a ledger, all of the related transaction will become perpetual. It charges a very minute amount to miner (especially on newly gained coins). Another process which gives actual meaning to the coin is commonly known as mining process or proof of work system.

The Composition of Crypto currency

While seeing rules of the crypto currency, some exceptions were also made which purely based on various factors which yonder the basic levels. These factors differentiate financial system from that of crypto currency. As given below:

Adaptive ordering:

There is numerous measure which ensure the proper functioning of crypto currency in terms of both small and large scales.

Sample of Adaptive Scaling:

Bit coin takes ten minutes for mining of each single transaction block. Recently in 2016, algorithms alter to timing for smaller or larger blocks to be mined. Suppose let it takes 13 days for the networking of 2016 blocks to be mined then it depicts that it can be mined very easily which ultimately enhance its difficulty. Contrary if it takes more than 13 days suppose, 15 days for networking of 2016 blocks then its depicts that it's too mine which shows that difficulty lessens.

Numerous other measures are incorporated in case of digital coin for adaptive scaling. It includes techniques of scarcity, like preventing the supply overtime. Also demotivating the loots for mining so that more total coins can be mined.

Cryptographic:

This system if particularly use for check and control on the creation of coins and to authenticate transactions. It is called as AKA encryption.

Decentralized:

Most of the time the currency is under control of the government which can also be delimited by any third party. On the other hand, the Crypto currency is an open system which is highly depend upon interconnect network and controlled by codes. No other external factors can control of effect the currency.

Digital:

Crypto currency is generally known as digital currency. The outdated models are represented by physical articles like USD, gold etc. digital coin are transfer by digital means and kept in digital wallets. It's all done electronically, no physical items are exchange.

Open Source:

Crypto currency is termed as open sources because any one can create APIs free of cots and everyone is allowed to join this networks or use it by any legal mean.

Proof-of-work:

All crypto currencies mostly utilize proof of work system. This system comprises of easy to verify and hard to complete computational enigma in order to decrease misuse of crypto currencies mining.

Most importantly, the given catpcha are really difficult to solve as it demands a lot of figuring powers. Alike this system another system is also very useful such as proof of stake is also used.

Pseudonymity:

The digital coin is kept in encoded digital wallet. Identification information of coin holder is kept in form of these codes. It does not carry person's identity. It creates a pseudonymous relation between coins and holder of coins instead of mysterious relation and are open to public. Ledger are used to assemble information related to groups of networks.

Chapter 02: 18 Effective ways and strategies to trade cryptocurrency to earn million bucks

Cryptocurrency Trading Overview

The foreign exchange of cryptocurrencies is known as Cryptocurrency Trading. This provides you with the facility of trading altcoins and bitcoins for BTC and USD. Thus we can say that foreign exchange of cryptocurrencies is another way to enter the dynamic world of crypto. You need not spend huge amount of money in bitcoin hypes, bitcoin cloud mining and there is no need of mining hardware, as all these are a bit risky.

Getting started trading cryptocurrencies like Bitcoin

To begin with bitcoin trading, the most important requirement is a wallet. If you have a wallet then you can safely purchase and protect cryptocurrencies as ethereum, bitcoin etc. if you are not a bitcoin holder then you must follow the instructions given on the guide to get one.

Security: To keep oneself protected is the dire need of everyone in every case. You must take precautionary measures and stay careful to keep yourself away from any mishap. While trading you must activate two-factor authentication to keep yourself protected. Majority of the foreign exchanges proffer you bitcoins (like: bitcoin for lite coin or ethereum for bitcoin), keeping this in consideration you must have bitcoins before you think of cryptocurrency trading.

1. Understand the Power of Cryptocurrency

Let us now talk about stock investing. Cryptocurrencies and Bitcoin are not stocks but commodities. Both of these have different prices as compared to one another but they can be exchanged easily. It is known that the technology that powers Bitcoin has inherent ability to be selected as retail capital and institutional. The meaning of decentralization of cryptocurrency is that it is not easy to close it or control it shrewdly. Majority of the people have different questions in their minds related to the purchase of Bitcoin. The answer to their queries is that as now the capability of Bitcoin is known and it is expected that it will bring advantages in near future so everyone should have a positive approach towards it.

2. Target and stop when starting a trade

The golden rule for trading is that you must set a particular target level as well as stop-loss level. A target level helps you earn profits and stop-loss level lowers the chances of risks. Stop-loss level can be defined as the loss level where trade is finished.

The task does not finish after setting a stop-loss level, you also have to take into consideration a number of factors while selecting a particular stop-loss level. When a trader develops immense love for the coins or trade, they let their emotions lead them and they ignore the daily variations that continue occurring in stock exchange. This thing does not benefit them at all. This loss rate is extremely large for crypto. According to an estimate daily variations in stock exchange are 2-3%. It is commonly observed that the value of coin drops a lot in just few hours, as it may reduce about 80%. Keeping this in focus, no trader wishes to keep holding its coins and wait for the perfect time as time is not always in your favor.

3. Meet FOMO (fear of missing out)

A trader must not get over-excited while investing the money when the graph of stock market shows progress in fractions of seconds. In such situations do not rush to trade, act cleverly yet carefully. Your invested money allures you to play the game. Hold on! Be patient as it is the moment when majority of fake people invade to distract you. As the price in market is rising, the fake traders will also offer you their low-profit shares. You should be vigilant enough to discriminate the real ones from the fake ones. As when the prices are rising the majority of traders that bump in are the fake. They offer you their coins while the rest ones are waiting for the peak time that will result in huge profit.

4. Risk Management

The inside reality of stock market is very unpredictable. It falls with the same speed with which it rises so don't let your heart drive your wits. Play the game with your mind and do not wait for the big profit. Large number of small profits will lead to a bigger one. Use your tactics timely and wisely to become the winner of the game. It will increase the weightage of your portfolio. Keep waiting for the big catch may cost you lose the game.

Risk management is a factor that alleviates your portfolio to a greater extent so manage your dealing in small portions when the market is not in your favor.

5. Initial Investments

Dealing with Bitcoin, your investment is not prone to market risks. The price of Bitcoin is somewhat stable so you don't have to suffer greater losses. It allows to stick to your investments rather than hurrying towards trade. So it is good if you start your forex trading with Bitcoin. But it does not mean that you just focus on Bitcoin, you must have a good knowledge of other market trends as well.

6. The underlying asset creates volatile market conditions

The trade of Altcoin and Bitcoin is somewhat alike. The value of Bitcoin keeps on changing. It is not always the same. This thing can be easily observed when the prices of Bitcoin are rising or falling. As the value of Altcoin is concerned, it is totally the opposite of Bitcoin. When one increases, the other decreases. The times when the value of Bitcoin is changing at a faster rate are the times of extreme care. You must think before you leap in case of Bitcoin investments, as no one is completely aware of the future trends. It may benefit you or let you fall. The future circumstances are never clear. So you should work on small trades rather than investing on bigger targets or waiting for the right time to invest.

7. Hedge Your Bets

A number of opportunities come while trading with Bitcoin to gain maximum profit as it is long-term safe planning such as, while placing bets you must be 90% confident of your profit and just 10% risk factor. This indicates that you are confident enough that your bets will lead you towards the profit. This positive approach minimizes the risk factor to a great extent.

8. Altcoin Trading

During forex trading you must have an eye on coins other than Bitcoins like Altcoins. Altcoins are not of great importance among the traders as their values fluctuate frequently. Besides this fluctuation

Altcoin also shows a rapid increase in the profit graph. Every Altcoin serves a definite purpose and fulfils the specified needs. DASH, Monero and Z Cash are the heart favorites.

9. Beware of biased sources

Internet provides you with saturated information on cryptocurrency. But most of these are one-sided. They keep on telling the benefits of cryptocurrency, ignoring the major risk factors.

10. Find the average price

While starting your stock business carefully choose the type of cryptocurrency, then divide your capital in equal portions and invest at least one time in fourteen days. To calculate the average profit, you must have equal amount of money in each portion.

11. Set a limit and stop when beginning a new trade

While trading you must keep two checkpoints in view, one for target achievement and the other for risk management (stop-loss). It is necessary to set a particular stop-loss level so that you may end your trading when the risk of loss increases.

12. Don't overextend yourself when trading

While cryptocurrency trading you must limit yourself while investing rather than investing huge amount of money. Apparently it seems much easier to expand your investments but in reality it is an uphill task. As when the rates decline you will have to suffer great losses so it is advisable to limit yourself.

13. Follow cryptocurrency trading charts

A cryptocurrency trader must have a complete knowledge of trading charts. He must know how to analyze the charts and draw conclusions from them. This thing is of great benefit as it may bring lots of rewards for you in terms of trading.

14. Use A Trading Plan

Everything in life follows a particular routine. Before beginning trade as well as during trade, a trading plan helps you a number of ways. The importance of a trading plan can never be ignored. So you must devise a plan for your trading. You must keep your feelings, ego and emotions out of this plan as it will result in loss only. On the other hand, your plan must consist of risk and money management guidelines.

15. Understand Bitcoin's Influence on the Market

In the world of crypto Bitcoin plays the same role as to what U.S. dollar plays in the global economy. Both of these are closely linked to each other for their existence. In the crypto world Bitcoin has the central value. With the help of Bitcoin, you can do trade with other coins, so it shows that the trade of Bitcoin sets the graph of crypto world's stock market.

16. Are You a Long or Short Trader?

The key to success in crypto world is patience. If you are a long trader then you must purchase Ethereum, Bitcoin cash, lite coin, and Bitcoin and then keep holding them. In crypto world the mainstream exchange is Coin base.

17. Enable Two-Factor Authentication

This digital world is full of fake people. They are ready to grab the reward of your hard work. To avoid this, you must have two-factor authentication of each of your accounts. After signing in as per your routine, enter the code that is provided to you. Crypto world is full of hackers. If you enable the text option, the hackers will easily steal your information and use it against you and for their own benefits. They will misuse your account while sending fake messages to others, harming the good name of your company etc.

18. Don't Forget About Taxes

According to IRS taxes are levied on cryptocurrency as it is considered as an assist or a property. The payable amount of taxes is higher in case you cash out investment with the period of 1 year.

Investment in forex exchange and in these tokens is the same thing or other. They offer you the platform to grow your capital so be careful about market trends and risk factors. If someone has a better know how of fixing a problem, it should not be assumed that he can fix every problem. You should leave the world of forex trading if you're not a man of technology, especially the digital one. New concepts demand complete concentration but in case of cryptocurrency tis deep concentration makes you successful as it is quite easy at grass root level.

— Future time is of cryptocurrency and it will rule our world of soft wares. (Block chain tech).

Chapter 03: Mining of cryptocurrency

Having complete grip on the basics of cryptocurrency will earn you benefits. The more you work in the beginning the more rewards you get from mining crypto coins. In the beginning of 2009 Bitcoin was released, which is known as the first decentralized cryptocurrency. A whole new world of cryptocurrencies came into existence after it consisting of Bitcoin Cash.

Which Alt-Coins Should Be Mined?

You would have probably earned thousands of dollars, if you are one of the miners who started mining Bitcoins in 2009. But the loss you had faced through all these years cannot be neglected.

Bitcoins are beneficial for those people who are already expert in this game, but if you are a beginner and a small buyer then you must not begin stock exchange business with Bitcoins. The money you spend on investments and maintenance is too much that you cannot get the estimated profit when it comes to start with Bitcoins.

Whereas the script-based cryptocurrencies that prove beneficial in this regard are lite coins, Doge coins, and Feather coins. If a person begins with lite coin, he may easily get 10 dollars after investing 50 cents everyday through consumer level mining hardware.

Is It Worth It to Mine Crypto coins?

If you are fond of crypto coins and it is your hobby to mine crypto coins, then your hobby can bring you laurels as you might earn one to two dollars each day. These cryptocurrencies are much easy to mine, so a common man with a hobby of mining cryptocurrencies can easily compensate the loss of $1000 in just eighteen to twenty-four months. At the same time, you cannot look upon cryptocurrency as a secondary source of income. As it requires you to invest large amount of money and gives you somewhat less profit, for example you would earn just $50 each day after investing 3000 to $5000.

Set Reasonable Expectations

If you are determined to keep substantial money earned through cryptocurrencies as your secondary source of income, then you must focus on buying cryptocurrencies rather than mining them. However, if your aim is to earn just a few digital coins then you can go for mining.

The miners who are expert enough tend to keep their electricity costs at a low level of $0.11 per kilowatt-hour. However, mining with 4 GPU video cards easily costs you about $8.00 to $10.00 per day or $250-$300 per month. This cost varies with the type of cryptocurrency you are using.

Here the two things to be kept in mind are:

- The investment you do for buying 4 ASIC processors or 4 AMD Radeon graphic processing units
- The present value of crypto coins in market.

Rarely or occasionally might it happen that the type of cryptocurrency you chose may come close to the Bitcoin value. If this happens, that happens just one in a while then you would become a millionaire easily. But this happens just once in a blue moon.

How Crypto Coin Mining Works

To see how crypto coin mining works including script-based coins like lite coins, Doge coins, or Feather coins the following three points must be kept in view:

- You should always be available for mining as it is through computer called as 'verifying transactions'. Bookkeeping service should also be provided.
- Keep your income rate less.
- Spend less amount of money on your personal needs like hardware and electricity.

The Laundry List: What You Will Need to Mine Crypto coins

For mining feather coins, doge coins and lite coins you will definitely need these ten items:

1. A coin wallet. It is a storage chamber that helps you to store your money and keeps it protected.

2. A mining software, free of cost, consisting of stratum and combiner for example AMD.

3. You must be an active member of online mining pool. This pool is actually a group of miners who work together to earn more benefit and keep the income stable.

4. You must be a member of online currency exchange. It provides you a means to exchange your coins with conventional cash.

5. You must have a 24/7 internet connection, approximately with a speed of 2 megabits per second.

6. Setup of hardware in a properly ventilated and cool area like basement or air-conditioned room.

7. A particular computer designed for mining. If you cannot afford a new computer, you can make your personal computer a mining computer but then you won't be able to use it for your personal needs, so it is advisable to purchase a new one for mining. Your focus should be on computer as laptop or gaming consoles would not let you earn handsome profits.

8. A mining ASIC chip or GPU. You can purchase it of $ 90 if it is second-hand or of $3000 if it is brand new. This chip will serve the purpose of workplace for mining and accounting.

9. A ceiling fan that keeps on regulating air to keep your hardware cool, as heating up effects your working greatly.

10. You must not be curious enough as market trends keep on fluctuating daily. The miners who are successful in this field spend a lot of time in reading and understanding the skills. They keep themselves updated with new researches, then they apply their

knowledge in mining and earn huge profits. The miner who works hard definitely earns the reward.

Chapter 04: The Future of Cryptocurrency

A digital currency that is operated through advanced encryption techniques (cryptography) is called as cryptocurrency. Before 2009 cryptocurrency was only imaginary. It became real in 2009 after the launch of Bitcoin. Bitcoin continue becoming popular after it. But it earned great attention from media and became important among the miners in April 2013, when it was recorded that after billowing ten-fold in consecutive two months Bitcoin's value reached $266.the maximum market value that Bitcoin earned was over $2 billion. But this progress suffered a 50% loss. This loss aroused many questions about cryptocurrency's future, especially of Bitcoin. It was being though that will cryptocurrency gain as much importance as euros and dollars or will it be blackened out. The answer was hidden in Bitcoin.

Bitcoin – the Current Standard

Bitcoin is a type of digital currency that is made through mining process. This process is carried out through computers that are capable enough to solve difficult crunch numbers and algorithms. Now the speed of their creation is so fast that in just 10 minutes about 25 Bitcoins are create. It is estimated that till 2140 it will be capped at 21million. Bitcoin is a type of decentralized currency as well that uses advanced technology to perform a lot of functions like verification by different networks, processes of transaction and issuance of currencies. As Bitcoin is decentralized, so there is no influence or interference of government or any other operating system.

Decentralization makes Bitcoin entirely different from FIAT currency which is a centralized currency. FIAT currency is issued by the government's central bank only. As the bank supervises the issuance of this currency and all other things so there is no certain limit of the currency issuance theoretically. Indirectly it is the government that controls the issuance of FIAT currency and eliminates the errors to avoid currency failures. Whereas bitcoin is totally free of such influences. Due to decentralization the cost of Bitcoin is determined by the number of traders who are willing to buy or sell it. In addition to this if there occurs a failure in Bitcoin currency there is nothing to compensate the loss, whereas the government compensates the loss in case of FIAT.

Alternatives to Bitcoin

No doubt Bitcoin has earned great success and is most popular among the traders, some companies launched other digital currencies as well, and they are:

- ***Lite coin*** – In the present time this coin is regarded as the greatest challenger of Bitcoin. Lite coin was particularly designed for transactions that are done at low level. This coin was launched in October 2011. Charles Lee, the founder of lite coin said that lite coin is just like silver to Bitcoin's gold. Lite coins require just a simple personal computer for its mining as compared to Bitcoin which requires heavy horsepower computers. The maximum limit of lite coin is 84 million approximately it is 4 times Bitcoin's 21-million limit. The processing time of lite coin is 2.5 minutes which is one-fourth of the time required for Bitcoin's processing.

- **Ripple** – In 2012 Chris Larsen, a technology entrepreneur founded a company known as Open Coin. This company later launched Ripple. Ripple serves two main purposes; it serves as a currency as well as a system for payment just like Bitcoin. XRP is the currency component of Ripple. This is a mathematical foundation just like Bitcoin. With the help of Ripple network, you can easily transfer funds to some other user in the form of any currency within fractions of seconds. Whereas the transaction of Bitcoin requires much time approximately it takes ten minutes just for confirmation.

- ***Mint Chip*** – Cryptocurrencies other than Mint Chip are decentralized and they were not created by any government, whereas Mint Chip was created by a governmental institution particularly the Royal Canadian Mint. It is a smart card that is used for the safe transaction between chips and holds value electronically. Mint Chip does not need any personal information, whereas Bitcoin requires it. Mint Chip is backed by Canadian dollar, a physical currency.

The Future

In the present time Block chain is rapidly becoming one of the most quickly becoming one of the most expected technologies. It is thought that block chain will help to forward the society. Use of safe and decentralized systems will definitely reduce the risks of scams and hacks that are much popular today.

Block chain's most important app is with Bitcoin. We know that Bitcoin's value is not so constant but it is paving the way towards a digital, safe and data based future.

No doubt the future is of cryptocurrencies, but the point of importance is to work out the ways to cope up with this change. As less research is done on this basis most of the fake people as well as crypto experts are spreading rumors and excitement for their own gains.

It is not good to get over excited before the change as it may cost you millions later. But if you are confident enough then you must do research on it and get as much beforehand knowledge of the new technology as you can so that you may not suffer a loss in future.

As the technology progresses with time, the difficulties that we face today like scams and hacks with digital currencies it would be easy to tackle the problems in the future with advanced technology.

It is fact that as the cryptocurrencies are becoming popular with time is it compulsory to get scrutiny from the government.

Since the launch of cryptocurrencies the number of traders who deal in cryptocurrencies has largely increased but there are some that do not use cryptocurrencies. As it is much hard to deal with cryptocurrency only the traders who have know-how of technology will be attracted towards it.

If cryptocurrency want to play the lead role in stock market, then it must be greatly accepted by the traders. Moreover, it must have different qualities as it should involve complex mathematical rules so that it can be protected from scams and hacks. At the same time, it should be easy to comprehend for the traders. It must be decentralized with proper security system so that the currency may not be used for illegal activities like money laundering, smuggling and tax evasion. It can be though that in future cryptocurrencies might become equivalent to FIAT currencies. It can be predicted on the basis of Bitcoin's success as it will pave the way for other cryptocurrencies.

Should You Invest in Cryptocurrencies?

If you have a hobby of mining cryptocurrencies, then it can be looked as a great option to invest in cryptocurrencies as there are a great number of chances that you may suffer a loss. Cryptocurrency has no definite value; its value is determined by the merchants who are interested in buying it. So it is clear that the graph of cryptocurrency values can undergo rapid changes. It can reach the highest peaks in just a few seconds and at the same time may fall to the same extent. As on April 11 2013 the value of Bitcoin fell from $260 to about $130 in just 6 hours. If you are not strong enough to compete with such challenges, then you must invest your money in other areas. However, there are a number of advantages of investing in Bitcoin. The people who are in favor of Bitcoin will continue stating its merits whereas the people who are against it will continue telling the demerits.

Bitcoin's launch has opened a whole new world of cryptocurrencies. Irrespective of the challenges that Bitcoin is facing now, its immense success since 2009 has led to the creation of other cryptocurrencies like Mint Chip, lite coin and Ripple. There are a lot of confusions in this regard that whether cryptocurrencies will prove fruitful or not. But the answer to these confusions and queries lies in the success or failure of Bitcoin as it will determine the future of other cryptocurrencies.

Chapter 05: How big of market value on cryptocurrency, a little bit about the digital marketplace?

The world is now a global village and This is the era of information technology. There is nothing any field which is without technology. People are focusing on businesses and almost every business requires technology. with every coming day, innovations are continuously occurring and new technologies are coming. These new technologies remove the old and traditional ways of doing things.

We can count the number of benefits of technologies but this trend of coming new technologies one after another has a negative impact. These are coming with no time space that if one technology is being used in the market and you become used to it then suddenly after a gap of few months you face a new technology with small updating material so this thing disturbs your way of working.

In the field of business, new technologies are playing a very important role. Day to day transactions requires a quick simple and easy way which does not require much time. The world is going very fast due to which people never compromise on lengthy and prolong procedures. Ways of delivering amount or anything commercially and modes of payments all requires updated technologies.

When adoption merges with heavy and mass commercialization then invention does not remain, it becomes innovation.in the financial industry, Cryptocurrency is a new and emerging concept and the world is turning towards it. In coming few years, it will become an innovation.

Transactions or trading via a digital currency is now an upcoming trend. We can say it a Cryptocurrency which is based on the principles and rules of cryptography. In which all the information is coded and it is safe from any cyber-crime. With the help of this method, all the information and private data remain safe.

In the financial industry where Cryptocurrency is working very efficiently. it's all working is decentralized means that no single person has the responsibility to run.

All the working has done independently and rules are set by a number of a participant who is continuously working in a market and are observing ups and downs in the market and then set the prices of coins. These participants are involved in selling purchasing of coins and they set the value of Cryptocurrency.

As mentioned above that Cryptocurrency is a digital currency and it is working on the principle of encryptions which provide a great security to the data and this security is not for a single or special person it is equal for all whoever will use digital currency will get a same level of security to his data.

BI intelligence with their resources has searched out the reasons for Cryptocurrency that why many businesses are turning towards Cryptocurrency and why there is such rise in it and what will be its future.

Market trends of Cryptocurrency

As the different names of Cryptocurrency are circulating in the market due to its users, its promoters and enthusiasts of Cryptocurrency. For example, Gold of coming generation, Currency used in future for international businesses, a movement without burden etc. It will be more convenient for the user to carry it along without any extra safety and burden.

Digital currency is becoming very popular among many businessmen from last few years. Because it is weightless money and a safe way of a transaction in the business world. It has also the interest with regard as one of alternative money in the market as it exponentially grows and Bitcoin is considered as one widely used cryptocurrency of this era. A market is increasing day by day and users of digital currencies widen the economy of investment.

It is considered as first decentralized and digital currency that is peer to peer that increased diverse reactions with the passage of time.

Similarly, a number of advocates consider this currency as a mode of superior payment mechanism, I-e works separately to the control of the government and is one of secure traditional payment system that has revolutionized in the stagnant financial industry globally in money 'term. Its growth had the delicate concern about its legality control accountability and usage.

Market capitalization of cryptocurrencies

Since the birth of Bitcoin number of digital coins is entering in the cryptocurrency marketplace that has still targeted up to 900 cryptocurrencies that are accessible on the bazaar of Web's Digital currency.

Bitcoin is now considered the largest network i-e of block chain by market capitalization and followed by bitcoin Cash Litecoin, Ripple and Ethereum.

Block chain Technology & Cryptocurrency's Future

Cryptocurrency is now it's becoming thriving for the segment of financial industry instead of taking into consideration the negativity that is surrounding it. It is also mysterious and unusual payment method that penetrate most unusual locals of already existing transactional world (online or offline).

As unexplored and unusual nature of cryptocurrency, government and investors are curious and worried about these illegal activities and are more concern with security-related with utilizing unregulated cryptocurrency.

In case of worrying about the susceptibility of currency to theft or any fraud, central banks along with government are taking it seriously about any loss of having no control over the regulation & money supply if it became the norm (digital currency).

There exist factors that let cryptocurrencies intrude in practical life and now it is indulging in our economy, as apart from apprehensions.

- One of potential outcome related to the mass adoption of different payment systems like bitcoins is for the purpose of providing businesses with the impetus to improve services.
- Similarly, the technology block chain is depicted as future of the economy as technology can unlock sharing economy and help energize

by creating it less costly and work on an online platform.

- As cryptocurrency is more profitable so it has the power to minimize much more and all of the above associated annoyances.

- The charges you will have to pay while doing transactions is typical annoyances that is in the context of traditional payment method i-e credit & Debit card, checks and banks.

- Bitcoin is considered a type of digital currency.

- Cryptocurrency stays and grows with the help of slow mass adoption.

- With the freedom & anonymity, decentralized nature also coupled with o fees and the reason for this is to attract most loyalist customers toward this digital currency.

Also, many other reasons for cryptocurrencies that are ding alteration of the financial world economy and we better know about it and can foresee future with never-ending opportunities.

As bitcoin can develop the SIM cards and also the obsolete paper passports. It also has that sort of potential of sorting and saving a lot of sensitive data and that can enable security that modeled to make the digital passports and the main thing that is creating digital IDs that will be beneficial for upcoming future.

If we foresee near future of cryptocurrency that ranges from cut right failure and taking into consideration its temporary craze for filling a crucial role in new worldwide currency. Its answer lies in between the extremes and is dependent on the regulatory and legal configuration that end up with the utilization of currency used in that country.

Chapter 06: Different types of Cryptocurrencies

It is important to mention the widely used cryptocurrencies by buyers and sellers in the world economy. There are a lot of views about different types of cryptocurrencies. Here we discussing few important one that is mainly highlighted in our economy.

1. Bitcoin

Bitcoin is very renowned in this economy as it is gaining much popularity our market with a lot of consumer spending their investment in this digital currency because if its demand in the economy. This is inspired bitcoin named as altcoins & it tried hard to exhibit themselves as more modified or along with the improved version of Bitcoin. There exists a tradeoff, having more risk bought within by less liquidity, value retention, and acceptance. So, the prices of bitcoins are mounting the heights, as we consider the six-important selected form 700 that can be worthwhile. It is not the only trendsetter that is in the wave of cryptocurrencies design on decentralized peer to peer network.

2. Litecoin

As it was launched in 2011 and is one of initial cryptocurrency and is referred as silver to gold bitcoin and was developed by Charlie Lee, who was MIT graduate and is the former engineer of Google, a very famous and most commonly used search engine. This cryptocurrency is founded on an open sources payment network that is not in the control of the central authority and is using "Script" as authentication of work that can be decrypted by the help of Computer Processing Unit (CPU) of Customer Grade. It has resemblance with bitcoin in the number of ways as it has quicker block generation rate and is offering fastest confirmation of a transaction. There are a lot of dealers who prefer and accept Litecoin other than the developers.

3. Zcash

It is open source and decentralized cryptocurrency that was launched in 2016 that appears promising. "If bitcoin uses "HTTP" for money than Zcash uses https" i-e how Zcash defines itself. It is offering selective transparency and privacy of doing transactions. In resemblance with https, Zcash claims to offer extra privacy or security where all the transactions are published or recorded on block chain but details of recipient, sender & remains private. They are offering customers with shielded transactions that enable content that can be encoded using the zero-knowledge proof construction or advanced cryptographic technique that is named as ZK-SNARK made by its team.

4. Ethereum

It was developed and launched in 2015 and is one of a decentralized platform of software's that let Distributed applications and Smart contracts to run and built without any sort of downtime or any fraudulent is possible, control or interference by the third party. During the year of 2014, It also launched pre-sale for the ether which received the overwhelming response.

Its application is working on its specific platform cryptographic token that is either. It is a vehicle for affecting around on platform of Ethereum and is an observation by a number of developers who are focusing on developing and running applications that are inside the Ethereum. Ethereum can also be "codify" secure, decentralized and trade.AS according to the occurrence on DAO in year 2016, and Ethereum was then split into Ethereum Classic (ETC) and Ethereum (ETH). It has great market capitalization of about 14.4 billion dollars that is worth much.

5. Dash

It is also named as Darkcoin and It offers anonymity and is working on a more decentralized master code network that enables transactions almost untraceable. It was launched in 2014 and dash experienced a number of fans that are using this cryptocurrency in the shorter period of time. It was basically developed by a creator of dash Evan Duffield it can be mined by using GPU or CPU. Darkcoin was rebranded as a dash that means digital cash and work under Ticker-Dash, in 2015.

This rebranding have-not changes its features that are technological i-e InstantX or Darksend.

How to avail them

It will be more difficult and tough to know that where to initiate and start and when you are going to take your first coin. It is easy to purchase. It carries different and many cryptocurrencies and there is no need of having a number of accounts for holding different coins. A few sites have selected to integrate larger coins which are present today. All sites which are alfacashier and crypts as well and on Coin base for bitcoins.

Although many and different ways of obtaining cryptocurrencies that will be described in the article. Don't forget to deal with sites or people upon whom you can have easily trust and in order of not losing money in case of any fraud /scams.

Just follow the instruction that we recommended and take a proper guidance from the mentioned site without getting into any sort of trouble or difficulty that might disturb you while doing work on it. Let's have a careful overview of how easily you can buy cryptocurrency for yourself.

Open cryptocurrency Wallet

The initial and first step the consumer might take for ordering and be able to hold coins and it is for the purpose of opening wallet of cryptocurrency. The number of choices of wallets depends on whether you are going to hold the coins-Litecoin & Bitcoins or holding different types.

These cryptocurrencies hold their own wallets that can be downloaded from a website and can be used for doing mine for coins. The work can be fine if we can go for the planning of having few and different coins due to which you will have different wallets at a time. Selecting this sort of wallets to minimize the options of purchasing coins through the exchange of cryptocurrency without proceeding for having another Wallet. No matter that which wallet you prefer to open as it by providing with a unique address of wallet where the people can go for sending you, your coins by ensuring that you will get them and have-not possible that these coins go to another person.

Using Coins form the exchange of crypto-currency

It is the most safer and unique way of purchasing the coins and using cryptocurrencies exchange site is more convenient for consumers to buy coins.

If you select trusted and large cryptocurrency exchange site, it will ensure you not only that money is very safe but also it enables fast and very secure transactions. So, it's necessary to do a careful view of selecting the people who have positive intentions to work with you to prevent any fraud or wastage of time. All of you must take very few minutes to do, it is just to select secure website of your choice and make an account over there. It takes less time of doing registration that can occur less than the few minutes and is fast and very secure to begin.

Further, you have to do for buying any coins is uploading of funds to cryptocurrency account that can be done through regular payment such as bank transfer and credit cards. It takes few minutes for the transfer of money and to the several days as it depends on a method consumer selected so there might sometime consume in the beginning of buying because sometimes it can happen instantly.

After the money sent to your account that you are now able to proceed toward the next process of purchasing coins. This is the last & final step of gaining access to the process of purchasing coins This process is easy as you have coins that you demand the selection of cryptocurrencies that you prefer to buy and you have to select how much coins you want to purchase and upon which prices you would pay to get it. Once upon the decision of all these things you will go for placing an order in system and exchange site of cryptocurrency will match the requirements with the coin's seller have and then deals may happen.

It might take few minutes or few hours that depends on the coin's price or amount that you have selected. So, the processing of order started and the system has selected seller according to your preferences for you. So in this way, you will get the coins in your wallet account as soon as possible and hence deduction of money from your wallet account occur and is then sent to that person from whom you are purchasing coins. Then you can do that you need to do with these coins that you finally purchased from the seller using the exchange site of cryptocurrency.

You can go to these mentioned sites for purchasing coins and these are fastest and secured sites for purchasing of cryptocurrencies. The reason of using these websites are that with the access of this website you can do safe and secure transactions a number of websites are build based on frauds that only hinders the activities of buyers so we enlist these websites for the convenience of consumers to go with secure transactions with the sellers and purchasing of securities that they want.

- Alfacashier.com
- Coinbase.com
- Cryptsy.com

Purchasing of bitcoins through Forums and Online Communities

Similarly, there are a lot of different ways to get cryptocurrencies by using online communities which pay importance to cryptocurrencies. So, in these communities, there are a lot of people you will find that are taking interest in the selling of coins to other consumer's different time for a price that has resemblance with market value or maybe a low value that they already have.

Purchasing of coins via the communities is a very simple way as in this way you are directly linked to the seller and can get detailed information about coins. It includes that how much coins you are going to buy the prices for these & paying user that money upon which you agree on. Upon finalizing you will have to give the seller the address of your wallet and then you will receive that coins in your Account. It will take almost 10 to 15 minutes after sending of coins to your account address.

You must be informed of few things that need to be in consideration while you purchased coins through this way. And the very first thing you must focus on is you should go for trading with only that user who has some references to any earlier trades that are not in case of any previous problem. The main thing why you consider it is that it will let you away from any fraud that you can send money to the seller and in return he will not send coins in your wallet that couldn't happen but it happens and Secondly, you must ensure that value of coins haven't gone down during which you are in dealing with the sellers. Because if it is happening then you are involved in the bad deal with in your purchasing process. If you try to follow this little advice so then you will be far away from having fraud or having the bad deal and can receive coins as fast as above your imagination. Instead of buying it through the cryptocurrency exchange rate.

Purchasing of Coins from Friends

It is the last option the consumer can entail with is buying the cryptocurrency from your own friends that are holding enough of coins that you prefer to purchase. Similarly, it is also a very secure and easy way of purchasing coins and all that you have to do is just figuring that how many coins you are in need of and upon which price you want and paying of coins' fee through the way you friend prefer.

Once it proceeds then your friend will be able to send you coins as per your desire to your account an and you can go for using the coins instantly or within an hour.

Another reason of buying from a friend is that you are fully aware of about your friend and you will trust them in this case because using internet technologies are not as easy to chase rather than purchasing of coins by your own friend of whom you know very well.

Chapter 07: Whether these currencies similar to Cryptocurrencies or not?

A very quick overview at most widely traded cryptocurrency news sources unable to present that impression. Their coverage presents impressions that people are of having a keen interest in trading of cryptocurrencies through the way as we go for the trading of other securities mostly of stocks.

It is uncommon in the circle of cryptocurrency to have a discussion of cryptocurrency as mean of investment some predictions about the explosion in future prices and might possible that it would constitute few of "Success" or proof.

Bitcoin if were primarily currency then the only measure of success might be adoption by sellers and buyers of services and products. Volatility, either it is negative or positive influences against that usage. It also makes it more dangerous for the merchant for using bitcoin, instead of exchanging it for the national currencies while every transaction that misses point of currency. For example, if a merchant sells about $4000 Us that worth for 1 beer for BTC and then one BTC becomes worth of $2000, it means that the dealer has lost about $2000.Similarly, if a merchant invests one bitcoin in $4000 that is worth of grain and he plans to sell at price of $8000 in near future originally one bitcoin would be the worth of about $16000.that's why it is an assumption that deflation frightens economist as much as they are afraid of investing. So, it has surprised that merchants are going away from this instead of opting it.

According to the perspective of traded security of there is an instrument that is already existing that has a resemblance to cryptocurrency so it is a penny stock.

Cryptocurrency as penny stocks

For different cryptocurrencies, the leading and important data service like coin market capitalization that is currently in the list of about 800, although they are not actively traded), as no one uses them for transactions of currency type. They act as a vehicle for the speculations. A very ambiguous story about the uses as a currency but in them, the interest is based on prospects of becoming richer and gaining more wealth as much as possible within a limited time.

Ethereum that is much touted but a project that is not a bitcoin which is considered to be "decentralized organization" and "Smart Contracts" attract attention to system token 'performance. That is technically named as ether to differentiate it from Ethereum block chain and it has been taken on very same name resulting in the main driver in block chains i-e Speculations Vs Wealth Accumulation.

Similarly, ICO is created only to parallel IPOs. An IPOs occur when a company goes public by offering ownership over many stock' shares that are named as equities as they offer a share of ownership in the company. ICO do something by distributing tokens by passing financial elites of which the promoters of cryptocurrency hate. But some ICOs may not offer a stake of ownership in the company. ICOs They run into exact SEC rules that they ignored.

Instead of these similarities, cryptocurrencies are not stocks as they are very honest to the goodness currencies. It is a stock-like investment as how we value them like the way by which we value stocks. Instead of frequent claims by promoters, there exist very little and long-term relationships among the price of cryptocurrency and else in this world.

The similarities between the cryptocurrencies and the stock are focused by promoters of cryptocurrencies within the context of what they named as market capitalization that is comprised of the number derived by multiplying the number of tokens with the circulation by its selling price. The market capitalization of cryptocurrency is easy to find and is the most familiar concept from the perspective of stock investing but not the currencies. It has some definite purpose as it is a rough measure of the size of companies. S&P 500 is comprising of an index of about the 500 publicly and largest traded companies sorted by the market capitalization.

If one person has every single bitcoin or if every bitcoin which is currently traded? What would be able to do it? As far as it is a concern, absolutely nothing about it.

Basically, the market capitalization has a very crucial role in the corporate finance. A stock is for the representation of ownership of a company. It offers the direct mechanism to do that, buying shares of stock. hence you own that company by means of which is called a tender offer.

In a tender offer that is simplest, a majority of shareholders are willing to sell a company for the set price.so the purchase offers to all existing shareholders. From the perspective of technicality, the shareholders get the right for the refusal of selling, As the company is acquired it is doing out of business so then the shares of its stock can become less worthy than before.

Market capitalization is the important factors in the stock pricing. If there is a fall in the stock price that is the possibility that the company may purchase by the competitor. Everyone will pay attention to number i-e it means something.
So, there is no parallel among this phenomena and market capitalization in the cryptocurrencies.

Chapter 08: The Block Chain Technology and Its importance

It is very much important technology. Organizations are increasing day by day and they have to focus on exploring the upcoming revolutionized technology that will be important for their business. Arc Andreessen who is from the well knows VC firm Andreessen Horowitz call it as a very innovative.

Many Organizations explores its possibility of block chain that is still in the financial service industry. In this the r3 consortium of biggest 45 financial institutions that are investigating what actually block chain meant for them. Also, 4 of biggest global banks also developed USC i-e Utility Settlement Coin is the digital counterpart and each of major currencies that are backed by central banks. The main objective of which is to develop or go for creating a system that undergoes transactions in real-time. Another example is Australian post, who have released plans for creating block chain based electronic voting system for Victoria's state.

How Does Block chain work?

Block chain enables business to perform efficiently and will also affect our lives. But the question here is what it is and how it works and why it is important?

The block chain is a shared single version of truth about things that are digital. It is called as database technology or a distributed ledger that managed data records that are decentralized. The data records that can be of bitcoin transaction or may be smart contract etc. are joined in so-called blocks. And adding these blocks to distributed ledger it is important to validate data by 51 percent of all computers that are within the network having access to the block chain.

Importance of block chain

Block chain, on its own first take into consideration the imagination of cryptocurrency enthusiast and bitcoin versatility of that technology that embraced experimentally by most well-established sectors of a world economy.

If it is compared with the traditional database technology and with the centralized systems, it can be cheap and require less IT investments to manage or maintain them. Similarly, as the technology is not much mature so these savings on operational cost may balance development costs.

Its application has established a lot of interest from the financial sector. Steps taken include cryptocurrencies that are modeled on bitcoin and on self-executing smart contracts that can implement different financial contracts. A very high-profile initiative is R3, the consortium of 70 financial institutions that was launched in 2015 and develop the block chain technologies for their use in the financial sector. Its application is creating tamper-proof records different initiatives proposed for a public sector that maintain registries implemented as block chains, for example, block chain tracing of donations from the donor to recipients to enable money goes where it was required.

The enthusiasm for block chain hasn't declined between technologies that have pushed the boundaries of this technology. Financial Institutions are also exploring self-executing smart contract technology .by pioneers of block chains. The launch of Dao i-e decentralized autonomous organization was very effective venture capital that was implemented by smart contracts without having resourced to a traditional legal structure in May, 2016.

Chapter 09: Ways to store cryptocurrency

As cryptocurrency has become popular among the masses, so it is the first priority to keep your coins safe and secure. In every situation and field the most important thing is security. Due to the popularity of cryptocurrency among common people, it has become easier for hackers to cause damage. The risk of scams and hacks has largely increased.

The most noticeable bitcoin exchange of the world appears to be a recreant entrepreneurism. However in reality Mt. Gox was just a combo of ignorance, immature experience, and improper management.

The people who were familiar with the working of Tokyo-based Company were extremely surprised when it went through failure seven days before, the misplacing of four hundred and sixty million dollars and loss of another twenty eight million dollars through the deposit accounts. According to the insiders, this company was actually a shadow of its Chief Executive and Mark Karpeles, many share bearers. Mark Karpeles was not a perfect chief executive. In reality he was an expert computer coder and was ignorant of his major duties. One of the Mt. Gox insider says that Mark loved his job as a chief executive but not its hectic routine.

It was published in a disclosed paper that Mt. Gox exchange was raided by hackers last week. Karpeles admitted this and said that a large amount of money was lost. He also said in a press conference that was conducted in Tokyo about the bankruptcy that their system had many faults and they suffered much loss. A number of people had to face many problems so I apologize for all this. So the exchange had an authorized access twice. About $8.75 million were stolen in June 2011. (Wired, 2014)

The Categories of How to Keep Your Cryptocurrencies

You can keep your cryptocurrencies in the following categories to keep it safe.

Online VS offline:

- Keeping cryptocurrency on computer, exchange or mobile which has a good internet connection is considered as online.

- To keep the money more secure people tend to store their money in a paper wallet or a computer that has no internet access. The other safe storage is in hardware wallet. The key of this wallet is in the hardware and is without any internet connection. This is regarded as offline.

Keep them yourself VS other party is keeping them for you:

- Keeping your cryptocurrency yourself means that only you know where the money is stored.

- Keeping your cryptocurrency on an exchange or on a wallet that is linked with internet means that you are involving other parties. In this way these parties also have an access to your money.

To deal with these situations carefully you first need to keep yourself well aware of all the methods by which you can store your cryptocurrency safely. But before this you must have proper know-how of the methods that can be used to keep your cryptocurrency. A small description of these methods is given as under:

Exchange: An online market that provides you with the facility of trading your cryptocurrencies; altcoins or fiat currency is known as exchange. An exchange that deals with cryptocurrencies consists of some crypto, you must have multiple types of coins to keep your name in the market. A reputed exchange today is coin base. Exchange can be regarded same as pocket cash. Enter this link: https://www.coinbase.com/join/593b0777d0 ff9b08bb0ace8d, sign up and get $10 for free.

Online Wallet: The software that has a good internet connection 24/7 and can be used for altcoin storage is known as online wallet. Generally we regard any particular thing that has internet access as online. In technical terms, there is no physical storage of coins. A wallet owner has a secret number, regarded as the private key of the wallet. The wallets that are connected to internet provides you with the facility of trading your coins. In addition to this it also shows the remaining coins to the owner. There are 3 major kinds of online wallets: web-based, desktop and mobile. The other type of online wallet is hardware wallet and it provides you greater security. You can easily find online wallets of similar kind and advanced security features at Blockchain.info. Online wallet is just like a Checking account, where you can buy and sell coins and it also keeps you updated with your remaining balance.

Hardware Wallet: A wallet with internet connection that is used to store cryptocurrencies and the wallet whose private keys are stored in a separate device, hardware is called a hardware wallet. These hardware wallets have more importance over software wallets like a wallet or an exchange with internet connection. The private keys of hardware wallet can never be transported out of the hardware device, as they are stored and protected in a microchip of the hardware wallet. There are almost zero chances of the hardware wallet being hacked. The only way of losing your hardware wallet's data i.e. cryptocurrency is by the loss of that particular hardware only. A hardware wallet is like a bank account. Among all hardware devices, the best one is Ledger Nano S. If you want to learn detailed information about this wallet then go to this link: https://www.ledgerwallet.com/r/73c4

Paper Wallet: A wallet that has no internet connection and helps you to store your altcoins is known as paper wallet. It is also called as cold storage. Key to this wallet is either public or private and is in the printed form on metal, paper, or plastic. This printed paper is stored in flash drive drive, or is written by hand on a paper. Offline wallets are considered more secure as compared to online wallets. Paper wallets are regarded as the most secure wallets until they have no internet connection. If you have no previous knowledge of creating paper wallets you can have an idea about it by going through these tutorials:

For Bitcoin paper wallet tutorial visit– https://www.coindesk.com/information/paper-wallet-tutorial/

For Ethereum paper wallet tutorial visit– https://hackernoon.com/securely-generating-and-storing-an-ethereum-wallet-907bcbd8e5ae

After getting the information about the methods of storing cryptocurrencies we must look at the one which can serve the best purpose in this regard. Some people are interested in the trading of all types of coins so for them it is necessary to provide them with all types of coins. An account of exchange is good for the people who are involved in small scale and everyday trades. If you want to send money to your family members and friends, want to trade at a larger scale, and want to pay your bills then you must have a wallet with internet connection or a checking account. If you want to keep the money of funds safe and secure then hardware wallets are best for it. If you have a large amount of money then you can look at the option of paper wallet, otherwise never ever think of it. Regardless of this, you must choose the one of your choice. Stand on your own decision and that will prove to be the paragon.

Chapter 10: Track the market, when to sell, when to buy, platforms and tools to use

Track the market, when to sell, when to buy

The stock market traders are much confused about trading Bitcoins. They are not sure about whether to trade Bitcoins or not.

The most important coin among the cryptocurrencies is Bitcoin. On Dec 7 it had a record of $17,000. Recently it was being traded around $15,000. This year its value rose to 1,550%. Since it suffered a low in January 2015 so now it is 6,540% up. Every cryptocurrency is making a new record each day, due to this some experts say that cryptocurrency is just like new gold.

However here the question arises that whether Bitcoin, Ethereum and other digital currencies are real or are just fake. Moreover there is also no authentic information about initial coin offerings. Initial coin offering is actually a crossbred of initial public offering and crowdfunding that has engendered Ethereum and other projects. It is suggested to Wall Street traders to trade and invest carefully.

In a Wall Street Journal it is stated that Goldman Sachs (GS) is considered as a cryptocurrency trading operation. On Dec 8 JPMorgan Chase (JPM) CEO Jamie Dimon said that he remains highly skeptical of the cryptocurrency. In September Bitcoin was referred to as a fraud by Dimon. He also said that cryptocurrency would be used in black market.

In 1840s gold rush, many people got into it but only a few were able to become rich. In August Bitcoin market hit $150 billion just like 1840s gold rush. Its value fell to $5,500 in Nov 12. In late Dec 8 it was being traded at $15,800.

According to UBS, one of the major risks is that the government might restrict the usage of cryptocurrencies, keeping them far away from mainstream like limiting its usage for paying the taxes. The Chinese government has banned the initial coin offerings and trading of digital currencies. Other governments can also follow these footsteps. However some retailers are willing to deal with Bitcoins like Home Depot, Microsoft, Subway, and Target. In addition to this there are multiple uses of digital currencies.

Cryptocurrency Investment Vehicles

Some exchange traded goods and a number of ETFs can be bought through cryptos and bitcoins. One of which is Grayscale's Bitcoin Investment Trust (GBTC). The assets of GBTC are $2.5 billion. This year GBTC is 1,250% up.

The launch of Bitcoin futures in the coming years will open a whole new world of cryptocurrency investment vehicles. The trading of futures by CBOE will begin on Dec. 10, and after that CME on Dec. 18. Due to the non-availability of futures the filing of Bitcoin's ETF creation by ETF provider, Van Eck's SEC was drawn back.

Increase in the value of Bitcoin was no more than a blessing for Coin base. Coin base is an exchange that deals with the trade of crypto coins and helps to store the coins in wallets. Bloomberg reported that on Nov 2 within 24 hours Coin base added more than 100,000 users after the announcement of Bitcoin's futures plans by CME Group.

According to Street.com in November Reality Shares NASDAQ Block chain Economy ETF was offered to file by ETF provider Reality Shares that in long term there will be investment in those companies that will provide more chances for block chain technology, so instead of keeping your assets it is beneficial to keep the futures going. The science behind cryptos and Bitcoin is block chain technology. Horizons Block chain Index was filed by Horizons ETF Management and Amplify Block chain Leaders ETF was filed by Amplify ETFs in November.

Bitcoin Vs. Gold

The cost of gold bullion in the current year has increased up to 8%, according to SPDR Gold Shares (GLD), which is an ETF. This increase in value is much less as compared to the cost fluctuations of Bitcoin. Due to the rapid changes in the values of Bitcoin the internet searches for Bitcoin has exceeded the searches for gold.

However the values of cryptocurrencies are vulnerable to changes. This year the cost of cryptocurrencies remained higher, Bitcoin's value suffered a 28% loss and it fell from $2,682.59 to $1,938.94 on 12th June. On September 1 its value sharply dropped 35% i.e. from $4,950.72 to $3,336.41 on September 14.

CNBC reported UBS analysts' research that instead of making a real world transaction with cryptocurrency, most of the buyers seek risky benefit. There is very limited usage of cryptocurrency in the real world. The Bitcoin transaction by block chain software is total opposite to the transaction that is done in a bank or real estate company. In routine bank transactions a middleman is needed to confirm the authenticity, whereas there is no need of a middleman in case of lock chain software as the software provides the required security on its own. Thus block chin software helps you to have secure, rapid and cheap transactions.

The transactions and money transfer via cryptocurrencies and block chain is done anonymously so people living in the areas where transfer of wealth is limited are much fascinated by this. It is said by the detractors that cryptos also attract tax dodgers, drug dealers, and money launderers in addition to authorized investors.

Bloomberg reported that Coin base is involved concerned in a case, the main purpose of which is to avoid IRS attempts to examine the accounts of the customers for taxable gains that are not reported.

How People Invest In Digital Currencies

People who are interested in buying and selling their cryptocurrencies on their own or by hand can perform this act by simply going to an exchange. The exchanges that serve this purpose are: U.S.-based Coin setter, London-based Bits amp, Coin base, Bulgaria-based BTC-e, and Cryptsy.

Cryptos need wallets to store their money and keep their private keys protected. Well-known exchanges provide their customers with soft, or hot, wallets. These type of wallets are for desktop computers and mobile devices. According to Coin desk they are like Xapo, Bitcoin wallet, Block chain, Mycelium.

Hard wallets that are in the form of devices like flash drives, and without internet connection provide you with extra security. You just need to connect the device directly to your mobile or computer. According to Buybitcoinworldwide.com, Ledger Nano S, Keep Key and Trezor are the most important wallets. You must learn the password by heart, do not forget the place where you kept the device and continue backing it up on daily basis to keep your cryptocurrency secure.

It is said that block chain technology is real and provides you with excellent security whereas wallets are at the risk of damage. A user lost $280 million of Ethereum ether coins when by mistake he deleted the access code provided by Parity Technologies. After July 20, all multi-signature wallets that were created by Parity were affected by freeze.

On December 31, 2016 Ethereum was at $8.03 but now it is 5,628% up. On December 8 it was at $459.99 and then its value increased to $464.99 the next day.

On September 6, Coin IRA founded Digital IRA Bundles. Coin IRA is a unit of digital currency. This was done by financial companies to bring Bitcoin to investors. The values of the bundles were like $25,000, $50,000 and $100,000. They were packed with digital currencies. There are three type of portfolios and each investor can select the one of his own choice, such as: aggressive, moderate or conservative. The bundle of conservative type consists of Ripple, 50% Bitcoin, lite coin, 41% Ethereum and 3% each in Ether classic.

Cryptocurrency Investing Like Juggling Chain Saws?

The director of global ETF research, Ben Johnson, situated at Morningstar, said in an interview to IBD that "direct investment is more risky as compared a diversified ETF that has some access to cryptocurrencies. "These risks are in comparison with the risks of juggling knives as compared to the risks of facing juggling chain saws.

SPDR Gold Shares or iShares Gold Trust and other exchanges of this type do not deal with traded funds. Grayscale Investments' Bitcoin Investment Trust, allows trading at the counter. This trust was founded on May 4 2015. An application was submitted by Grayscale to SEC, seeking for the permission of trading GBTC on NYSE Arca. But not being a well-managed trust, Grayscale drew the application back on September 27.

A recent premium trade of GBTC was 44%. There is no proper system to keep NAV and the price within certain limits, however Morningstar Direct lists GBTC with its ETFs.

From August 31, GBTC shares were down by 54%. But then it regained its original value, even now it is 1,500% up. It again suffered a 20% loss on September 1. It happened when a short-seller Citron Research said that GBTC was the most risky way to get Bitcoins and the trade of Bitcoins must not exceed $550 per share.

Eric Balchunas, ETF Analyst with Bloomberg Intelligence, told IBD that Bitcoin Investment Trust trades at high premiums so it is not an easy way to trade as you will suffer damage in every type of situation. In contrast to this investing through ETFs is a fair means of dealing and trading Bitcoins.

Proposed ETFs In The SEC Review Process
In March SEC rejected Winklevoss Bitcoin Trust due to improper regulation and fluidity. Over the previous three years, ETF candidate is under consideration by the officials.

On September 27 Pro Shares Short Bitcoin ETF and Pro Shares Bitcoin ETF were filed by ETF provider Pro Shares with SEC. Both of these ETFs wish to chase the contracts of Bitcoin futures rather than getting the currency. Van Eck also drew back his 11th August application on that day, for Van Eck

Vectors Bitcoin Strategy ETF, that was concerned in Bitcoin's futures investment.

Fidelity Investments with Coin base is trying to step into the field of cryptocurrency. On August 9 Fidelity's innovation unit declared that from now on Fidelity customers can check their Bitcoin, Ethereum and lite coin balances in their wallet accounts. In the upcoming two years Balchunas will put the odds at about 50/50 of a new ETF option.

He said to IBD that since the rejection by SEC two key developments have occurred since March. One of these developments is a regulated Bitcoin futures and options markets. The other is the changing of SEC in addition to new administration. The new head of the division of investment management who represented the Winklevoss twins' Bitcoin filing was previously a lawyer at the same workplace.

Other ETFs with Cryptocurrency Exposure

Todd Rosen bluth, CFRA's Director of ETF & Mutual Fund Research, told IBD that the fluctuations in Bitcoin's value are much more than other currency based investors and products in an ETF wrapper. ARK Innovation (ARKK) and ARK Web X.o (ARKW) in addition to access to Bitcoin, have more traditional equity investments for Amazon.com, Tesla and Twitter, lowering the risk factor."

ARK Investment Management was the first ETF to have GTBC shares, and it now owns 6 ETFs. According to Morningstar Direct, ARKK with 83% gain and ARKW with 80% gain were the first two ETFs on December 7. ARKK was launched in Oct. 2014 and since then it has gathered assets of $295 million. Whereas ARKW, which was launched in Sept. 2014 has attracted $193 million. ARKK and ARKW bear an expense ratio of 0.75%. There are many Kinetics Mutual Funds that have their own GBTC shares. Two of these are: Kinetics Internet

(WWWFX) and Kinetics Market Opportunities (KMKNX).

Investors must never ignore the potential risks while dealing with virtual and cryptocurrencies. According to Zen Cash co-founder Rob Viglione, "as the theory suggests that if market prices retain any useful informational content, then the 10x run-up in the crypto market capitalization over the last year indicates that an important thing is going to happen." But it is not clear that whether the thing is speculative or radically transformational.

Top 5 best tools and platforms for getting started trading the bitcoins:

Inexperienced traders are easily caught up in the traps. They are not aware of when to trade, when to buy and when to sell coins. You must have a complete knowledge of these five tools to trade Bitcoin.

1. Set up trading accounts on the best exchanges

The selection of a perfect exchange plays the most important role. A good exchange helps you to earn handsome money whereas a bad exchange leaves you empty handed. You may predict the ruination of an exchange before investing.

Coin base – The easiest way to buy Bitcoin

Coin base is a trustworthy wallet that helps you in buying and selling Bitcoins. It has collected more than one hundred million dollars in fund raising expedition from angels and VC's. It is so easy to deal with Coin base that even a common man can trade cryptocurrencies with it. Your Coin base account rapidly links with current account and so you can trade money and transfer it with much ease.

Bitfinex – A very liquid exchange with the ability to short Bitcoin

Bitfinex, a perfect place for shorting Bitcoins. In the beginning it had some issues but now it is a trustworthy workplace for new and active traders. Due to U.S. dollar trading it is ranked as a top exchange.

Poloniex – The best place to trade altcoins

Poloniex, known for margin trading and shorting on many altcoins.it is relatively a new exchange. It is best for trading Ethereum. Poloniex is capable of catching Ethereum's first massive bull market.

Key Point – Don't trust exchanges to act as your bank

Trade with bitcoins is still not safe from scams, hacks and damages. Many of the Bitcoin exchanges have undergone bankruptcy, have suffered unauthorized access, or have stolen their customers' digital currencies. Exchanges are commonly known as the area where you can easily buy, sell and trade your coins, but they are not as safe as a savings account. Most of the exchanges are seaward and they do not provide you with the insurance facility at all. So it is highly recommended that you must not keep your cryptocurrencies in the said exchange.

2. Use the best charting tools

If you desire to become a vigilant trader, then you must have a complete knowledge of tools required for booking order and the best charting. Coinigy is the best tool in this regard. It comprises booking order and charting and order execution for each type of digital exchanges and currencies. It also serves the purpose of trading platform. There is also a facility of linking your accounts to Coinigy. Then you can place orders easily and chase your trades in a particular area. They are fully equipped with tools that are needed for technical analysis. There is a beautiful charting interface also.

3. Set up mobile charts & alerts

In the busy world of today it is totally impossible to sit in front of your computer the whole day long to check Bitcoin charts. Sometimes a situation arises when it is totally impossible to keep a check on all the charts. The best solution to this query is that you must set mobile alerts so that you can easily check them through your smartphone.

A mobile app called Zero Block serves this purpose very well. So what you need is to just download the app in your smartphone and keep yourself updated.

4. Move your trading profits offline into cold storage

Exchanges are not a good place to keep your cryptocurrencies. Cold storage is a secure place to store your coins. As described earlier in detail that cold storage refers to a wallet that has no internet connection. There is no risk of hacks or scams in offline wallets. One of the best cold storage tool is Trezor. It is a type of hardware wallet for Bitcoin storage and provides you with extra security. You can choose any cold storage from a number of cold wallets like paper wallets, computer wallets and hardware wallets... the most important thing in this regard is that you must know how to keep your money safe and secure.

5. Join a high-value trading community

It is generally observed that most of the traders suffer a loss in trading. It may be due to a number of reasons but the most important one is lack of education and training.

You may consider trading just like any other game...As you may not win any of these games without particular techniques and strategies in the same way you cannot earn profit unless you have a complete knowledge of trading. After you have completely learned the techniques and strategies that are compulsory for trading, the next step that you have to take is to definitely join a trading community. When you become an active member of the community you will come to know about the latest market trends, when to buy and when to sell. In a community you learn from the experiences of traders as they share their real life experiences so you better know that what are the risks in trading and in what ways you can earn maximum profit.

Chapter 11: Mistakes to Avoid When Trading Cryptocurrency

Crypto-Quora is a platform where you can ask a number of questions related to cryptocurrency and get a number of replies from experts or cryptonians. One of all those questions there is an important question comes to mind that what are the worst mistakes of beginner and how to resolve them. When you share it on the Crypto-Quora you can get many replies form cryptonians. So, with the help of this platform, there is a list of mistakes which beginners of cryptocurrency make and that must be avoided to keep the work smoothly.

1. Not believe in mediums, Do research by yourself

This is the biggest mistake which many people ever made. A number of people rely on different mediums, they mostly spend a lot of time on social networking sites, like Facebook, Twitter, and many others, you share your problem there and get many replies from number of people there is a possibility that they are also the beginners and they don't have any experience. So, if you are a beginner and you do not have enough knowledge about cryptocurrency than instead of asking on different social networking sites do research by your own way and find that what's the reality in it and how a number of things are working in it then get a guidance from an expert of cryptocurrency. Do work by yourself that when to sell and when to purchase coins. If you will totally rely on others, then you will lose all your money and nothing will remain in your hand.

2. Do Not Expect a Big Profit in Very Start by mining.

Expecting a big profit at very initial level is not recommended to beginners. For the beginners, it is better to avoid it and firstly they should focus on their own research work which they have to make while investing in cryptocurrency. Although bitcoin miners are millionaires behind this they have a lot of their work and time they have spent. As a beginner, you do not need to start mining because for this you need expertise, large-scale investments, and hardware. It will not be profitable for the beginners who are working on smaller scale.

3. Don't be impatient

It is very important for the crypto users to be patient and do not be very quick in response to some news. Beginners do not have much experience and they usually make a mistake while being impatient. As you, all know that and listened that patience rewarded the best. So, do not quickly sell or purchase any coin with every coming news. It is like a stock market where with every coming day prices fall and rises.

If you have a plan, then with the patients stick with it and do not sell it for a short period of trading. Check its rate and them do work according to it.

Warren Buffett says that there is no difference between stock market and cryptocurrency in this respect that both are like a transferring machine by which you can transfer money from an impatient to the patient.

4. Sell your crypto when it is at a high price.

It is a common mistake that crypto beginners make. they sell their crypto a price which they are considered a high price and when a price goes about that price on which you have sold then except regretting you will never get anything. So, while selling your crypto make a plan and check a trend of prices then sell it.

5. Being unknown to your private keys

It is the biggest mistake you ever do it. Being unknown to your private keys or not holding it will give you a huge loss. Private keys are the way by which you can save your amount in your account. If you do not hold it then how will you secure your account?

6. Not having a good community for learning

It is a mistake commonly beginners do. They do not find a good community from which they can talk to those people who have enough expertise and skills. If you talk about good and learning communities then your knowledge will enhance, you will be more motivated. You can get support from such communities. These are the names of communities from where you can get your answers while talking to people

- SingularDTV Slack
- r/ethtrader
- Decred Slack
- Crypto Twitter

7. Sending crypto fund to wrong address

Beginners do this technical mistake and send their crypto details to the wrong address but it is not a big problem it can be fixed easily.

For avoiding this problem, when you send tokens then check it twice that to which exchange wallet you are sending or transferring a fund. Send it to the right exchange wallet. Sending Bitcoin to an ETH wallet is not appropriate so does not send it. Sending OMG to the CVC wallet is also not ok so does not send them there.

When multiple tokens are ERC20 then you can send them to MyEtherWallet but not to the exchange wallet.

8. Not keeping passwords in hard copies

Don't commit this mistake it will have severe impacts. You have to save your documents or passwords, your private keys in a hard copy. In case if your computer or software crashes or hacked, it will be a proactive approach and can work as a backup for you. You can restore your all data within time.

9. Not saving records related to the codes

Not saving records related to the codes or not using two-factor or two-step authentications is a big mistake which most beginners commit. Due to this mistake access to your account by any outsider will be very easy and your whole data can be easily stolen. It is for the security of your identity. Because of not using this method and not saving a restoration code you cannot unlock your account and for unlocking you have to ask it to the customer support service provides to unlock your account.

10. Fear of Missing Out

This mistake is very common which newcomers do. Many people invest in overhyped ICOs and want to earn lots of money even though they do not know about the technology. So, you do not worry about the past opportunities of ICOs which have missed. With every coming day, many new opportunities come in the world of cryptocurrency, do your research and avail them.

Carefully take your steps

In the cryptocurrency's world, every path is full of thrilling and terrifying risks. Where every step should be taken with full attention and carefulness. This is the game of risk takers if you consider yourself a risk taker then you can play this game and you cannot end this game before starting. these risks will give you another experience.

This is a world of extreme complexity where beginners can fall because they do not have experience of moving the path of this world. They most of the time do not understand altcoins and due to lack of experience and the missing informing will become the cause of their fall down.

Chapter 12: Best Approaches for Beginners and advances while Trading Cryptocurrency

Best Approaches for Beginners while Trading Cryptocurrency

If you want to enter in the world of cryptocurrency, then the first thing you have to know is what is cryptocurrency? Cryptocurrency is a new and emerging concept and the world is turning towards it. Transactions or trading via a digital currency is now an upcoming trend. We can say it a Cryptocurrency which is based on the principles and rules of cryptography. In which all the information is coded and it is safe from any cyber-crime. With the help of this method, all the information and private data remain safe.

Cryptocurrency is a digital currency and it is working on the principle of encryptions which provide a great security to the data and this security is not for a single or special person it is equal for all whoever will use digital currency will get a same level of security to his data.

The feature cryptography has made it attractive in the whole world. It is not run by Governmental bodies. BTC, Bitcoin is it's an important and vital digital asset which is followed by Ethereum.

Cryptocurrency Exchanges

Next thing which a beginner must know is Cryptocurrency Exchanges. It is a platform through which trading of digital currency takes place for dollars or euros or any other currency. It is a platform through which coins and dollars are exchanged. Bitcoin can be sold and in exchange for that Bitcoin you can get a dollar or in another case, you can exchange ether for Bitcoin or vice versa.

There are two types of exchanges exist. One is a public exchange and the other is a private exchange. Private exchanges are exclusive and are operated by one company. Some exchanges have very flexible norms and by which digital assets can be easily traded via messengers, telegram etc.

Choices of Cryptocurrency Exchanges

The next question after Cryptocurrency Exchanges must be that what are the things which must be considered while choosing cryptocurrency exchanges.

There are some features which you have to keep in mind while choosing the best exchange for trading needs. Those features are mentioned below

Fees

You must be familiar with the fee structure of the specific exchange. Because every exchange has some fees for which they are providing you a platform for doing business. Research about the fee of cryptocurrency exchanges in your own way and then choose the best option of exchanges.

Verification Requirements

Before starting a work over any exchange, you must know that what is the requirement of signing up to that exchange account. Then you have to fulfill those requirements. These requirements are related to your identification, details of your passport and driving license, residential proof or any other document related to these proofs. They take all the information for the security purpose. When the complexity of verification process becomes more than exchange platform will be safer.

Exchange Rates

The third thing you must know is exchange rate at which you can sell or purchase your crypto. If you don't have any idea about exchange rate, then it will never be a fair game for your business.

Reputation

The world of cryptocurrency is like a stock market where fluctuations will occur at every coming moment. And the cryptocurrency platforms must have many ups and downs. But these ups and downs will never hit the reputation of best exchange company or traders. they have strong reputations and fluctuations cannot easily bring a point towards their reputation.

Region

Considering a region is also an important thing. It is very vital to choose that exchange which will provide a support regarding your geographical locality. In some regions like South America, exchanges will support but it is not necessary that at everywhere same exchanges will support you. So, choose the best option for exchange while considering your locality or region.

List of cryptocurrency exchanges

It is your responsibility to choose the best platform for the cryptocurrency. Some are as follow

Coin base

It is a plate form which provides you secure online trading facility. With the help of which you can sell or purchase, digital currency. You can transfer digital currency to the other accounts. You can avail the backup facility via this platform. It is world renowned online trading platform having users more than 4 million and it supports you in 32 different countries. If you sell or purchase a Bitcoin then transaction modes can pay pal, credit card or a bank account or via another channel.

If you want to start a work on coin base, then you must have an e-wallet. It is used for the purpose of purchasing or selling of your crypto.

There is a certain limit for holding Bitcoins. For the residents of U.S, that limit is 50,000/day. Coin base is a well-reputed exchange company in the trading community. This company gives you a value by deducting only 1% transaction fee .it is other than that fee which you pay depending on the selection of your payment method.

When you register with the Coin base then you can use another exchange named as GDAX which is also in the ownership of coin base. GDAX has some more features which will help you in Market Limit, stop orders, and margin trading. GDAX offers very low fees.

Local Bitcoins

Local Bitcoin is an exchange platform which is widely used in many big cities of the world. It works on the principle of trading via a local currency. With the help of local Bitcoin exchange, you can post advertisements, payment methods for buying and selling of Bitcoin and you traded it among locals in local currency. You can purchase digital currency via a bank account, PayPal, and square. This exchange platform has a fee deduction of 1 % but in those cases when as a seller you apply your exchange rates.

As a local Bitcoin trader when you apply rating it will be displayed to the public. When you are transferring a fund, or doing transaction then check all the ways for the security purpose. 1 percent commission is given to local Bitcoins.

Binance

It is another exchange platform. A number of cryptocurrencies are available by which you can easily trade. It has a very reasonable fee which attracts you towards it. Due to its attractive features, you can register and it has no prolong and lengthy procedure so you can easily get into your account without verifying your account. After that, you can make withdrawals that are about 2 BTC/day. It is becoming famous among people because its speed is effective, it is very easy to use and has a very low fee.

CoinMama

The largest brokerage of Bitcoin is CoinMama. You can purchase coins via your debit card or via a credit card. It has a low transaction fee. as compare to CoinBase, CoinMama has a greater limit of buying Bitcoins. the range on which you can get $5000 of coins/day to $20,000/month. For working on CoinMama you have to make your account. After that, you will get the details on the page of your account about Bitcoins that how much you can sell or purchase and select your mode of payment. Also, add Bitcoin address and your contact details. When you will complete your verification process then you will allow getting Bitcoin via a CoinMama.

CEX.IO

The world's oldest platform of cryptocurrency is named as CEX.IO.it is used for only trading pairs of alt-coin named as Bitcoins and Ethereum. For purchasing other currencies CEX is used and with the help of Changelly, you can convert them into other crypto.

CEX.IO has a registration with FINCEN. It works on the principles of KYC and AML. If you want to work on this platform, then it requires verification of your identity before trading. This platform will entertain you regarding the use of credit cards, SEPA and wire transfer.

This platform will give you convenience that when you will start your trading it will calculate r count the transaction prices and freeze the rate of exchange for about 120 seconds.it has some hidden fee which is 7% of fiat currencies. Means that if you buy $100 bitcoins then you will get only $93 in coins.

Best Approaches for Advances When Trading Cryptocurrency.

The trend of cryptocurrency is booming over the whole world but many people do not have an idea that how to participate in this upcoming trend of digital currency. Due to lack of experience and knowledge beginners fall down. Many people do not know about Bitcoin so ow will they operate or work with cryptocurrency.

There is some important tip for the beginners which are listed below

1. Research your interested altcoins

Research everything in your own way is the first thing which everyone will suggest to the beginner. Do not rely on others. As a beginner search on different websites that what updates a cryptocurrency has mentioned. They have a separate website for altcoins. Dedicated Slack and Reddit forums are available for public discussion where you can ask quarries and get replies. By this way, you can resolve your confusions and clear our concepts.

Many people are investing in overhyped ICOs and they want to earn lots of money even though they do not know about the technology. So, you do not worry about the past opportunities of ICOs which have been missed. This is the opportunity for the companies which are holding ICO's. They take the advantage from investors. ICO is a way by which you offer some new cryptocurrencies in exchange for a Bitcoin or any other cryptocurrency. It is a way to raise money and not a secure way so do not lose your money in overhyped ICO's offerings. Research over the technology, team or community which is authentic. Protect your investment and invest after research. For example, Siacoin, Dash (DASH), Zcash (ZEC), Monero (XMR) etc.

2. Do research on trends in market

It is very important for you to conduct a research on market trends of altcoin and analyze them that on what rate and market cap it is trading in the market. Update yourself by visiting different sites like coin market cap. From where you will know that what are the top cons which are trading now in the market at highest rates. You can check an indexing site named as Cointube where you can invest in top listed 20 coins. Research on market trends and increase your information. This will be beneficial for you and for your business.

3. Trading Bitcoin in exchange against altcoins

After doing a research number of options will be in front of you and thinking about all those options will help you to take a good decision and choose the best option. You can trade your coins by using an exchange like Bittrex. It all depends on you that how much you are interested in your money to generate a good profit from it. For example, the worth of Antshares were only $4 / piece before 4 months, you invest and purchase 100 coins, when it is rebranded and named as NEO then it's worth and value reached at $42/ piece. So this all happens due to your research and being updated on the market trends. When you analyze it, you make a perception and work according to it.

Bittrex is very useful and good exchange, via this platform you can exchange Bitcoin with other altcoins and trade them. Bittrex is the largest crypto exchange. In which exchange occur from one crypto to another crypto. It is very secure exchange with 2-factor verification process. It has a trading fee of about 0.25% but has no reduction of an amount in it on withdrawal. Cryptocurrency is market wherewith every second, fluctuations occur. So if you are a risk taker and have the ability to lose and can bear a loss then you can invest in it. Otherwise only thinking about the profit is not a good approach.

As cryptocurrency is a new and emerging concept and now it is widely flourishing around the whole globe. Due to Ethereum, the decentralization of applications and internet is getting very fast. It is not as like Bitcoin but there are many differences lie between them in terms of their capability and purpose.

Bitcoin is associated with an online cash system while Ethereum is associated with the deployment of decentralized applications. An emerging concept is prevailing in the market of cryptocurrency is that Bitcoin and altcoin work opposite to each other. When the price of Bitcoin increases, the value of altcoins goes down. This happens because with the increase in the value of Bitcoin traders make an exchange of altcoins against Bitcoins. And due to the availability of a huge number of altcoins makes them devalue. Oppositely the same thing happens with the Bitcoin when its value goes down the value of altcoin increases. These trends are very important to understand if you are investing for short time term.

Bitcoin is a digital currency if you purchase it then you have to hold it for some period of time. But if you take Ethereum, then it is different in the working and has a different purpose too. With the help of Ether coins, you can hold a property and make payments via Ether coins. This brings a convenience regarding the paper contract and payment procedures.

There is a question comes to your mind that how to get Bitcoins. This becomes very easy now, you do not need any lengthy procedure. By ATMs deposit, your amount and Bitcoins are deposited to your wallets. You can use different exchange platforms like Coinbase and Coinmama, where you can purchase Bitcoin via any payment method.

In the field of tech startups, cryptocurrency startups are new. A team with brilliant and skills are working on it. These startups are comprised of traction team of entrepreneurs, problem-solving platform, and revenue. If you are entering the world of cryptocurrency can participate by investing in them through purchasing altcoins.

Chapter 13: Pros and Cons of Trading Cryptocurrencies

Cryptocurrency's trend is getting very common around the world. a number of businesses are turning towards it. It has some positive aspects as well as some negative aspects. its pros and cons are mentioned below.

Pros

Cryptocurrency has a number of advantages like via cryptocurrencies transactions become more secure. It is weightless money etc. Some more advantages or positive aspects are mentions below.

1. Gives more time.

It gives you an advantage that patterns of cryptocurrency require some extra time to run. So due to which you can get more time to get more information you can process it analyses it and then you will reach a point where you can make a good decision. This is the difference of cryptocurrency with the stock that while trading in a stock market due to its volatility you will not get time to think overstocks and its trading. While in cryptocurrency you will get enough timeframe in which you can easily think over trades. It is an online way so via any devices a phone or tablet you can work over it while traveling also.

2. No time limits

You can do crypto trade at any time. There is no limit of a time period. It is available at any time for you. Whenever you want to trade you can, it's all depends on you. There is no restriction of time span.

3. Huge range

Cryptocurrency has a big range of intraday trading. Cryptocurrency offers you to take moves from 5-10% within few hours. Ethereum as well as Litecoin both cryptocurrencies have very good ranges on which you can trade.

4. No restriction of amount

This thing also creates a difference between stock and cryptocurrency that in stocks you are restricted to some amount on per day trading but in cryptocurrency, you are not bound to that amount limit.

Cons

There are some negative points associated with cryptocurrency. These are mentioned below.

1. Slow Moving:

In the world of cryptocurrency, it is very important for the crypto users to be patient. You have to wait for a longer period of time. If you are not patient, then it will be very difficult for you to work on it.

2. No Respite:

There is no respite in crypto trading. It is working 24 hours. You have to check your devices regularly even after every 5 minutes so as a crypto trader you will lose your sleep.so if you do not want to miss any opportunity then keep yourself ready for every coming situation.

3. Unregulated Market:

In the cryptocurrency's world, every path is full of thrilling and terrifying risks. Where every step should be taken with full attention and carefulness. This is the game of risk takers if you consider yourself a risk taker then you can play this game and you cannot end this game before starting. These risks will give you another experience. It is an unregulated market where every step should be taken carefully.

Chapter 14: Good resources for trading crypto currency

If you are new to investing crypto currency, you have to search out genuine resources for investment and realizing the capability of new ones. In the ocean of online information, you have to pick up the trust worthy sources, which is far more challenging being an investor.

Fortunately, the coin coaching is guiding you wholly. Following are given the most reliable resources to remain informed of varying investing trends of crypto currency:

Coin Market Cap

Coin market cap is one the most important that you must have to try. Once you buy a bit coin, you will frequently have asked about the next step of investment. A bit is just a beginning. You will see there are thousands types of crypto assets and crypto currencies.

Coin market caps categorize different groups on the basis of "market capitalization." It automatically detects the current prices as well as all related crypto currency exchange. Moreover, they depict the trading volumes and percentages of losses and gains for each crypto currency.

Although it seems very simple but it gives maximum details about the updates of changing marketing trends. It will enable you to apprehend more about assets and acknowledge you about necessary details.

Sub-Reedits

As per your knowledge, Reddit is vastly known and one of the most popular platform, which is comprise of sub groups for more specified topics, known as "subreddits". It works best in crowd source as well as for filtering noise from web information. As people update information and quality of post depicts the quality of community and people get attracted to what seems most interesting to them.

Some initiatives are given as follows:

- /r/BitcoinBeginners (all introduction about investments and bit coin technology)
- /r/bitcoin (overall discussion of bot coin).
- /r/ethtrader (ethereum & investment in crypto currency)

Each type of coin consist of its own kind of subreddit like r/ethereum, r/litecoin etc. it could help you to acquire all information regarding new coins.

YouTube Channels

YouTube is the hub of most appropriate information regarding cryptocurrency. Channels offer all type of technical and non-technical analyses. Like:

- Iva on tech (https://www.youtube.com/user/LiljeqvistIvan)
- Boxmining (https://www.youtube.com/channel/UCxODjeUwZHk3p-7TU-IsDOA)

You have to remain aware of deceiver, for this use mental filters.

Steemit

More or less it resembles reddit. It uses blog format which resembles voting system. You can post articles and rewarded with STEEM cryptocurrency. It is a blockchain projects resembling bit coin. It is categorized as:

- (https://steemit.com/trending/bitcoin) relevant to bitcoin.
- (https://steemit.com/trending/cryptocurrency) general information.

News Outlets

This is particularly for traditional news readers. Media outlets contains investing trends regarding cryptocurrency.

Most recommended are:

- CCN (https://www.cryptocoinsnews.com/)
- CoinDesk (https://www.coindesk.com/)
- CryptoInsider (https://cryptoinsider.com)
- CoinTelegraph (https://cointelegraph.com)

Chapter 15: Protecting the gain in trading to sustain and growth long term

Since the start of 2017, revolutionary changes are marked against cryptocurrency market. High return on investment is marked on cryptocurrency market. You will get x100 times more than your investment within 365 days. It is named as long term investing. Certain guides are provided for investment methods i-e long term cryptocurrency portfolio.

As per name, long term investment is take an account of investments for longer period of time. Unlike stock market where long terms meant for years, it takes few months or rarely a year. In stock market investment, warren buffet is most

140

prominent name who is an advocate deals with long term investments.

Proven by historic statistical figures of rising economy:

According to the S&P, more than 60% or returns is recorded in last 5 years. As per FTSE 100, around 25% return is observed. With the passage of time, the market trends are keep on increasing, on this basis mostly beneficial perceptions are made of long term investments. It is proved true for not only previous 5 years but also for every 5 years of economy.

Lower fees:

You must have to use an active trading method for prior investing and then you may expect some amendments in your profits. While implementing long term strategy, you have to choose some cryptocurrencies and then wait for outcomes. Usually long term investors, are not worry about trading fee as they prohibit daily trading.

Less risky:

If you visit market on and off, you may have deprived of significant gains. In case of long term investment strategy, you don't need to worry about this. You may use DCA method to get in touch wit h markets for reducing volatility.

After getting enough knowledge about long term investment strategy, now you have to choose correct type of cryptocurrency you wish to add in your portfolio.

Before this, let's take a look at some of the indicators, you can use to gauge the capability of crypto project in meaning of long term. Here they are:

Indicators of Long-term Value

Market share:

Typically, it defines the market capitalization of a cryptocurrency. Dominancy appears in the large market shares like, as per record, bit coin is having 60% market share of total market capitalization currently. It is particularly used to determine viability of long term crypto currency, including bit coin in portfolio.

Utility value:

If cryptocurrency will be introducing here in coming few years, you will definitely ask about its worth and its benefits particularly for users in market. They are very significant questions as in upcoming year, cryptocurrency will occupy the market. For instance, ethereum, its utility cost originates when it allows developers to build (DApps) Decentralized Applications in block chain. Hence it is concluded that as long as DApp will be used it will greatly enhance the utility costs. Consequently, etherreum will be worth enough to be added in your portfolio.

Transaction volume:

It is most efficient method of measuring uses of cryptocurrency. As per ethereum, its daily transaction volume is calculated as 500,000 ETH. It is proved form historic statistics that, this figure will keep on increasing as long as trends will restate in portfolio.

Technology development:

This is the key feature in terms of cryptocurrency. If technology behind cryptocurrency fails, ultimately long term strategy will also fail. Take an example of ethereum's current byzantim hard fork.it allows more transactions on ethereum block chain. That's why ethereum is getting viral with its increase positive technologies. So can make it a part of your portfolio.

Market news:

There might arise some serious problems regarding cryptocurrency which may immensely effect its long term practicality. Market news may affect the value of your portfolio, rates of cryptocurrecny.so you have to be prepared to lever them. Moreover, various other factors can affect pricing of cryptocurrency. It will help to remain up to date with market trends and news which may be helpful in terms of portfolio of cryptocurrencies and aid you regarding investment decisions.

Few indicators, will aid you to govern the practicality of long term strategy of cryptocurrency. While keeping all these things in mind, now you are able to construct an effective portfolio along with proper proportion of each kind of cryptocurrency.

Conclusion

Cryptocurrencies are becoming widely famous among many of the economists, futurists and even authors. But, what exactly is this? for few people, it is still hidden in veil and there are many secrets which are to be unveiled yet. Mani literature has been published regarding this technology, consisting of the basics of the cryptocurrencies along with the complete details of its trading and its types. Out of all these books, this book holds a special position because it not only covers the fundamentals and types but also predicts the future of the trends of cryptocurrencies and the market.

Being a simple and an easy guide to the cryptocurrencies, this book involves the complete details about the implementation of the technology of cryptocurrencies and its trading.

the book is dedicated to the deep understanding of this field with the elaboration of its trading, future, types, trends, and much more.

Understanding the mechanism and being involved in the business is necessary is a huge task and requires the complete concentration and affects the world of economy at a large scale.